# DISCERNING + RESPONDING
# TO PROPHECIES

## HOW TO BE MORE CONFIDENT
## ABOUT WHAT GOD IS SAYING TO YOU

Psalm 29

John E. Thomas

## JOHN E. THOMAS

# ENDORSEMENTS

I have spent the past twenty years raising awareness in the body of Christ as to how important discernment is. I actually believe it is one of the least used Gifts of the Spirit in use today. Because of this, I have seen believers be drawn away from Truth to deceptive error.

I am grateful to John Thomas in providing practical instruction on how to discern God's voice in the midst of prophecies uttered. If you have ever received a prophetic word and wondered how to apply it to your life, you will want to pick up this new book, *Discerning & Responding to Prophecies*. Thank you, John, for bringing clarity to a sometimes muddied issue.

**Dawna De Silva**
Founder and Co-Leader of Bethel Sozo International Ministry

There are books written that deeply carry eternal truths and there are books that carry a fresh word in season for the current conditions of our day. This is a book that carries both of these much needed graces and invites us into deep contemplation regarding the state of how prophecy is measured and left unchecked.

John's writing has the ability to invite the reader into a deep well of revelation through clear and simple language that moves past the intellect and addresses the heart and spirit. Chapter three addresses soulish prophecy in such a clear and profound way that it alone is worth the price of this book!

Having seen firsthand the devastation that soulish prophecy and mishandling the gift of prophecy has caused in the lives of sincere believers throughout my time in ministry, I highly recommend this book for all those who desire to grow in the prophetic.

**Daniel Burton**
Sent As One Ministries

In *Discerning & Responding to Prophecies*, John Thomas does a masterful job of helping people navigate the landscape of prophetic words. While prophecies can be insightful and helpful, they can also be either off-base or misapplied. Concerned with possible dangers, many people just ignore prophetic words altogether, but in so doing, they can miss out on powerful encouragement and guidance confirmations that prophecies can supply. John shares practical guidelines and principles that can validate legitimate words, keeping us safe. John's biblically solid and mature approach charts a course to embrace the truth of legitimate words. He also shares how to keep from falling prey to words that are off base, or from misapplying what we hear. This little book is solid gold for those who want to receive the truth from legitimate prophetic words while maintaining safeguards to help keep us out of trouble!

**Bishop Bill Atwood**
Anglican Church

*Discerning & Responding to Prophecies* is an invaluable guide for anyone navigating the world of prophecy. Authored by my friend John E. Thomas, president of Streams Ministries International, this book serves as a much-needed plumbline in a time where discernment is scarce and deception is common. Whether you're new to prophecy or a seasoned prophet, this book will equip you with the tools and wisdom necessary to operate in prophetic power while maintaining a life of purity. John's insights are not only enlightening but also practical, making this book an essential resource for anyone desiring to grow in their prophetic gifting.

**Justin Allen**
President/Founder Times and Seasons LLC

In a world where the pursuit of God's power often gets entangled with human flaws, John E. Thomas offers a compelling perspective on the need for genuine, authentic expression of spiritual gifts. His unwavering dedication to seeing the body of Christ operate in the fullness of God's power, free from personal agendas, shines through in his latest book. With a heartfelt focus on the significance of healthy prophetic ministry, John's passion for this subject is evident in both his life and ministry.

**Kristi L. Graner**
Pastor and Director of Dare to Believe Ministries

Published by Streams Ministries
PO Box 248, Lewisville TX 75067-0248
www.streamsministries.com

To contact John E. Thomas about speaking at your church or conference, go to https://streamsministries.com/invitejohn.

ISBN: 978-1-945771-07-1

Printed in the United States of America

# TABLE OF CONTENTS

# CHAPTER I

## WHY DO WE NEED TO DISCERN PROPHECIES?

# WHY DO WE NEED TO DISCERN PROPHECIES?

Several years ago, I was pastoring a church on the East Coast and met a woman I will call "Sarah." She was a worship leader, and though she had been a Christian for a while, only recently had God opened her eyes to the prophetic and other things of the Spirit. She began going to every prophetic meeting she could find—all the meetings we did at the church, plus whatever other meetings she could find in the area.

Then one day she stopped coming to church.

She had been so hungry for more of the

Lord, and I noticed when she wasn't there. As her pastor, I started to be concerned. Had something happened? I finally called her.

"Hey, what's going on?" I asked. "Where have you been?"

She began telling me a story. A couple of weeks earlier, she had gone to a prophetic meeting in the city where someone was giving highly accurate prophetic words. Clearly this man could hear from God. He was sharing extremely detailed words of knowledge with the group.[1]

But when he got to Sarah, he told her she was supposed to marry a man who was at the meeting. He pointed the man out to her in an obvious way, and Sarah was horrified, because she already knew the guy he was talking about. In fact, the guy had been pursuing her for a while, and she wanted

---

[1] A word of knowledge is one of the spiritual gifts listed in 1 Corinthians 12:8–11. It is when God reveals information the person giving the word didn't know through natural means. This could be information about someone's past or present.

nothing to do with him. They did not "fit" well together, and dating him was just not a possibility.

She told me on the phone, "If God wants me to marry this guy, then I can't trust God, because I don't like this man. I don't *want* to be married to this man."

Sarah did not have a grid for the possibility that this "prophetic word" wasn't actually from God. Though the prophetic individual had been extremely accurate with other people, he totally missed it with Sarah. This becomes obvious as we look at the fruit, or result, of his "prophecy" in her life:

- She felt like she couldn't trust God anymore.
- She was running away.
- She wasn't sure if she wanted anything to do with the Church, much less the prophetic.

Thankfully, as I explained how it is possible

for a prophetic word to be inaccurate, Sarah understood what I was trying to say. She was able to deal with that disappointment and still engage with God in a prophetic way—but now with more wisdom and understanding.

> Someone can give crazy-accurate prophecies or words of knowledge in one moment and then miss it the very next time they speak.

Stories like Sarah's happen all the time, and they are why it is so important to discern prophetic words. Is the word really from God? Or does it have another source? Words can be wrong sometimes. Someone can give crazy-accurate prophecies or words of knowledge in one moment and then miss it the very next time they speak. Just because someone heard from God a few times doesn't mean they heard from Him every time they thought they did. All of us are learning and growing, and this includes those who are known for their prophetic giftings.

How can we know with certainty if a prophetic word really is from God? That is what we're going to cover in this book. At the end of the book, you will feel more confident about the prophetic words other people give you, as well as what you are sensing personally from the Lord.

## "Prophecies" Can Come from Multiple Sources

When it comes to hearing and sharing prophetic words, Peter gives me so much hope. He was always putting his foot in his mouth. It is like he blurted out whatever came to his mind.

In Matthew 16, Jesus, Peter, and the other disciples were traveling through the country, and Jesus asked them, "Who do people say

I am?"

"Oh, You're one of the prophets," the disciples replied. "You're Elijah, or You're one of the other guys."

"Okay, but who do *you* say I am?"

Peter's simple response is incredible: "You're the Christ, the Son of the Living God."

Jesus Himself was amazed. He basically responded, "Wow! Flesh and blood didn't tell that to you. You didn't figure that out on your own. That was the Holy Spirit. The Father revealed that to you."

Peter heard God's voice and received a beautiful revelation of the Messiah's identity *before* the Messiah had fully revealed Himself. That is high-level revelation.

However, just a few verses later, Jesus was explaining how they were going to Jerusalem where He would be beaten, turned over to

His enemies, and killed.

Peter said, "No way. May this never happen to You!"

Jesus instantly knew that was not the Father talking. Looking at Peter, He said, "Get behind Me, Satan. You are not after the things of God, but you're after the things of man."

In one part of the story, Peter heard from God and knew who Jesus really was. But in the next part of the story, he somehow heard the enemy, and he tried to tell Jesus He was wrong. If that could happen to Peter— someone very close to Jesus, who knew Him face to face—it is certainly possible for people today to hear from God and give incredible, mind-blowing prophecies that are absolutely true. And then, a short time later, give a "prophecy" that is not true.

This does not mean the person is a liar or a false prophet. If that were the case, Peter would have lost his spot on Jesus' discipleship team, but Jesus did not write Peter off. Even after this event, Peter was still one of Jesus' closest friends. He learned from his mistakes and grew in maturity.

Well-meaning people can "miss it" with God's voice. We are human, and we make mistakes sometimes. Just as there was hope for Peter when he missed it, there is hope for prophetic voices today.

> **Just as there was hope for Peter when he missed it, there is hope for prophetic voices today.**

Knowing it is possible for a "prophetic word" to be wrong, we need to have discernment every time someone suggests they are speaking on the Lord's behalf. There is no reason for us to automatically assume something is from God, even when the person tells us, "This is what God is saying to you." Instead, we need to learn to recognize the word and its source. That is the subject of the next chapter.

# CHAPTER 2

# 7 WAYS TO DISCERN WORDS FROM GOD

# 7 WAYS TO DISCERN WORDS FROM GOD

Our relationship with God is more important than someone's prophetic word. One day when we stand before His throne, He is not going to ask why we didn't obey more prophetic words—He will ask how we obeyed Him.

First Kings 13 tells an interesting story. God gave a young man specific directions: "Go to Bethel and prophesy this. Don't stop to eat or drink, and be sure to come home a different way than you went."

The young man went to Bethel as he was told, delivered the prophetic word God had given him, and God backed it up with supernatural signs. An altar broke in half without anyone touching it, and the king's hand was withered and then healed.

After this astounding experience, the young man started home, but an older prophet who lived in Bethel stopped him. The older prophet invited him back to his house for a meal and refreshment, so his journey home would be more comfortable.

"God told me not to eat or drink in this place," the young man said.

The older prophet replied, "I also am a prophet, and an angel said to me, 'Bring him back with you so he can eat bread and drink water.'" But this was a lie (see 1 Kings 13:18).

The young man listened to the older prophet's "revelation" and didn't stop to speak to God about it first. This did not go well for him. Later on his way home, he was attacked and killed by a lion. He was responsible to hear God for himself and discern if this new "prophetic word" was from Him. We also are responsible for the words we receive.

So how do we discern if a word is from God? Here are seven ways we can "test" a prophetic word and discern more clearly if it really is from the Lord.

## 1. Who Gave the Prophetic Word?

When someone gives us a word, one of the first things we need to look at is the prophetic individual: who they are as a person, how they live, their nature and character, if they love Jesus and the ways of God, etc. When someone is antagonistic to Jesus, we don't need to listen to them. For example, if a witch, psychic, or palm reader tries to speak to us, it doesn't matter how "accurate" the word might seem—we can ignore it.

A person's character is so important when

it comes to hearing the Lord's heart and sharing what He is saying with other people. Every time someone tells us, "This is what God wants you to know," we need to take a look at their character.

Are they prone to insecurity or pride? If so, they will likely put more weight on the revelation than necessary, trying to convince other people it is accurate. A major thing to watch for is exaggeration. John Paul Jackson, the founder of Streams, used to tell a story about someone who supposedly had a high-level encounter with God. They hinted the Lord had visited them in person and given them a message. But after asking some questions, John Paul realized that wasn't the case. The person had felt the Lord's presence and had come to understand some things, but the experience was not the huge "visitation" they were implying.

Some people consider exaggeration to be a form of faith, but I cannot agree with that thought. When I first met the Lord, I listened to people talk about their encounters with Him and how He spoke to them, and I became confused, sometimes frustrated, because He didn't speak to me in the "big" ways He spoke to them. It took a while for me to realize these encounters were often much simpler than what the people described. Since then, I have tried to be specific about how revelation comes to me. If I *feel* something is true, I want the other person to know it is a feeling, not the audible voice of God. If I see a picture in my mind's eye, I want to say it is a picture, not an open vision in front of me. Exaggerating our prophetic experiences is basically lying—we are communicating something that is untrue as if it were true.

In addition to insecurity or pride, is the prophetic individual known for outbursts of anger or controlling behavior? Anyone who claims to hear God's heart needs to reflect

His heart; they need to be like Jesus. If their character doesn't look like His character, we don't need to listen to them

> **Exaggerating our prophetic experiences is basically lying —we are communicating something that is untrue as if it were true.**

Similarly, is the prophetic individual dishonest, or do they have a history filled with broken relationships? When someone doesn't understand the importance God sets on love and unity, but they repeatedly reject others or cut them out of their life, they can't be trusted as a bearer of God's voice.

How does the prophetic individual talk about other people and other ministries? Do they slander and demonize those they don't agree with, or are they able to love them despite those disagreements? Do they know how to challenge and correct in love, or do they make fun of those who are different than they are—perhaps in different streams of the Church or in different political parties? If a prophetic individual cannot love those who are different than they are, there is a chance their negative judgments will "filter" their revelation and turn it into something God isn't saying. Character is so important that if we can't trust someone's character, we shouldn't pay attention to their supposed revelation.

At the same time, however, I am not saying we should ignore prophetic words from people who don't seem "worthy" of His voice. Sometimes God will use openly unrighteous people to convey His messages. Maybe the person isn't living according to God's ways, or perhaps we know them personally and are familiar with what they struggle with. "How could this guy give me a prophetic word?" we might wonder.

Whenever and *however* God speaks to us, we need to have the humility to recognize His voice, even when it comes from someone unexpected. But we also need to have wisdom; He might use an "interesting" person to speak to us, but this doesn't mean we should start relying on that person as a mentor or always listen to everything they say. We should have a clear "witness" from God that it really is Him speaking, and then we want to take the time to filter out what parts were Him and what was opinion or pain coloring the message in a way He didn't intend. Ask Him for confirmation. "Is this word truly from You?"

The Bible is clear God can use strange, or even impossible, things when He wants to speak to us. In one Old Testament story, He used a donkey. The animal opened its mouth and started speaking in a human language that Balaam, its rider, could understand. Balaam was a magician, and he was on his way to curse God's people, which God didn't want him to do. Balaam was ignoring God's voice, so the Lord spoke through the donkey. The word was, obviously, accurate—despite the unusual vessel through which it came.

On the receiving end of a prophetic word, we also need to be people of character who operate in love. No one we meet in the prophetic arena will be perfect. We all have issues we're dealing with, and we all need the space to grow. It is possible to dismiss an inaccurate word *and* still value the person who gave it to us. Perhaps they didn't get it right this time, but God might use them in a brilliant way next time.

Here is a simple prayer we can pray every time someone gives us a prophetic word: "Lord, do You want me to pay attention to this?" Then we do what He says.

## 2. Is the Prophetic Word Scriptural?

One of the best ways to discern revelation is by giving it the Scripture test. Does the prophecy line up with the overall scope of God's Word? This doesn't mean we will find a "proof text" (the exact words or scenario) for every revelation, but the Bible clearly lays out certain truths about God's nature and His doctrine, and true prophecy will not violate His Word.

For example, Scripture says, "Every spirit that confesses that Jesus Christ has come in the flesh is from God, and every spirit that does not confess Jesus is not from God" (1 John 4:2–3). Based on this passage, we know any prophetic word that denies Jesus or how He came to set us free is not from God. He will not speak something that contradicts Scripture or the doctrine therein.

Our heavenly Father loves us and wants to talk to us about our life, and there are many things in the modern world that don't appear in His Word. He might tell us, "Move to this city," or "You need to relocate to this place," and neither of those places is mentioned by name in the Bible. Or He might tell us to buy a certain kind of computer or car; obviously, we won't find either of those things mentioned in Scripture. However, we *will* find in Scripture several different stories of someone receiving direction from the Lord. "Go here. Do this." These types of prophetic words are not creating new doctrine. They are simply giving direction.

In summary, God won't reveal in a prophecy something brand new about Himself or the way the spiritual world works, because that would mean revealing new doctrine that doesn't appear in Scripture. However, He will frequently talk about things that are not specifically *in* Scripture.

## 3. Does the Prophetic Word Agree with the Basic Tenets of Our Faith?

Jesus Christ is the only way to the Father. When we understand this truth, we start to recognize that certain well-known dreams, visions, and angelic encounters were demonic in nature and not from the Lord.

Muhammad's experiences came from a demon, not from God, because they contradicted what was already in Scripture. Similarly, Joseph Smith met with an "angel" called Moroni who also was not from God, because what the angel said violated Scripture. Any prophetic word or encounter that introduces an idea or concept antagonistic to the basic doctrines of Bible-based faith is not from God. Paul warned the Galatian church about this, possibly because there were people pointing to prophetic experiences and trying to introduce new doctrines (see Galatians 1:6–9).

Certain ideas aren't *necessarily* doctrine, but they are standard practice for the Church. For instance, God won't give someone a prophetic word that directs them to sin. Jesus clearly said in Scripture that God hates divorce. Based on that truth, we know He won't tell someone to divorce their spouse so they can be happy.[2] He won't tell us to murder someone, He won't tell us to steal, etc. In many cases, the Bible is clear about what is righteous and what is unrighteous, and the Lord will never direct us to do something that violates His righteousness.

If someone gives us a word that goes against the basic tenets of our faith in any way, we can know the word is not true, because God won't tell us the opposite of what He has already revealed in Scripture.

## 4. Does the Prophetic Word Line Up with God's Nature?

Whenever God speaks, the "tone" of His voice will fit His nature. He is abundant life (John 10:10). He is kind, long-suffering, and highly interested in our benefit (1 Corinthians

---

[2] We will talk more about this in the next chapter, but it is possible for a prophetic word to come from a person's soul and not the Holy Spirit. If we feel unhappy about something and then receive a prophetic word about how much God agrees with our unhappiness, it could be that we are hearing our soul. For more about this, read chapter 3.

13:4–5). He does not condemn us (Romans 8:1). He does not say things like, "You messed up, and there is no hope for you." Or "You've blown it, and I can't help you."

> **Whenever God speaks, the "tone" of His voice will fit His nature. He is abundant life.**
>
> **John 10:10**

God will speak conviction in a prophetic word, but He will not speak condemnation, because condemnation is not His nature. Condemnation says, "You're wrong. You're bad. There's no hope for you." But conviction says, "You did this wrong. You shouldn't do this next time, and you can change." One tries to strip out our hope and paint a negative picture of our identity. The other addresses an *activity* that needs to stop or change, because it doesn't line up with who we really are.

God will not manipulate or force us, so when a prophetic word is truly from Him, it won't be manipulative or forceful. It could be strong, but it won't use brute force to try to compel us to change. When He speaks, it is an invitation; He *invites* us to do something beautiful and draws us closer to His heart. True intimacy cannot occur under threat, and the Lord knows this.

The heart of God is welcoming, and He lovingly calls us to Himself. He is merciful and patient, and He is concerned for our heart when He speaks. As my friend Sarah discovered in the last chapter, God is not going to tell us to do something that will absolutely desolate us and leave us with nothing.[3]

---

[3] *There may be times when God leads someone to make a sacrifice, but in most cases, that sacrifice will not leave the person with nothing. Instead, it will become a seed that brings them a significant harvest later. The sacrifice might also remove something that is keeping the person from recognizing Him in their life.*

When we aren't sure about a prophetic word, we can compare it to His nature. Is the word loving? Does it line up with the fruit of the Spirit: love, joy, peace, goodness, kindness, faithfulness, gentleness, self-control, and patience? The words God speaks will always carry the fruit of His Spirit, because that is what He is like.

If a prophetic word is unloving or does not agree with His faithfulness or goodness, that word is not from Him. At the same time, God can correct us and will sometimes warn us of potential judgement. Jesus told one person, "See, you are well! Sin no more, that nothing worse may happen to you" (John 5:14). He warned the church in Thyatira that sickness and death would come to some if they refused to repent (Revelation 2:21–23). These words were clear warnings, but they carried the love of God, calling people into His purpose for their lives.

## 5. Does the Prophetic Word "Fit" You?

A prophetic word from God will relate to us

in some way. It will make sense for us at one level or another.

For instance, if we are not the president of the United States or one of the president's advisors, God likely will not tell us, "Go tell the president what to do." When He speaks, the word usually connects with our real life in some way. It will relate to something already within our wheelhouse, and it will be an action we could take or participate in.[4]

If God gives us a word about something that does *not* fit our life—we have no control over this thing, or we have no ability to perform or accomplish it—this could be an intercessory word. He might be asking us to pray. "Ask Me to move in this situation. Ask Me to open the door for the president or this nation, so the people can walk in My peace."

---

[4] *Sometimes people can have such a puffed-up view of their importance that they start hearing things that aren't from God. "I am called to direct kings!" Or "God says I'm going to be the senator's closest friend!" We need to hold our heart in the same place David did. He said, "I do not occupy myself with things too great and too marvelous for me" (Psalm 131:1). If we keep humility of mind, not looking out just for our own interests but also for the interests of others, having the same attitude and mind as Jesus (Philippians 2)—we will be able to hear the Lord more clearly.*

Intercessory words can feel "large" and prominent, but all we are called to do concerning them is pray. We don't need to worry about making the word happen. We don't have to figure out how to move things forward—or how to *keep* them from moving forward. If there is something else God wants us to do about this word (in addition to prayer), He will tell us, and the door will open at the right time.

God sometimes talks about "smaller" things that don't *seem* to fit us in the beginning, but they end up making more sense later. For example, perhaps we are interested in dancing, but every time we try to dance, we feel embarrassed because we're not very good at it. Then one day we get a prophetic word about how much God wants us to dance. That word, as unexpected as it is, could be genuine—because He loves our dancing, even though it makes us feel awkward. This is a very different situation than being told, "You are called to take charge of the president of the United States," when we have no relationship with that person. In most cases, God doesn't give prophetic words that do not match us.

## 6. Has God Confirmed the Word?

If a prophetic word surprises us and we can't see how it fits our life, but we think it might be the Lord, we need to discern the word's "price." How much would it cost us if we followed this word, and it ended up not being the Lord?

Here are a few questions that can help us determine the cost involved:

- If we follow this word, will we be embarrassed if it ends up not being from God? Embarrassment is not a high price to pay.
- If the word ends up not being from the Lord, will we lose a little bit of money? Again, that is not a high cost.

- How many other people will be affected by our decision to follow this word? Is there a possibility others will be hurt or severely inconvenienced? That is a much higher price to pay.

- Is following the word going to affect our relationships or the people we are responsible for? What does our spouse think of the word? How will the word affect our children?

God might say something that is completely out of the blue, but in my experience and observation, this is not normal. If we receive a prophetic word about something unexpected, and following the word will cause us or the people with us to pay a high price, we need to wait for a significant amount of confirmation *before* we believe the word is from God.

Certain direction words aren't a big deal. Maybe a prophetic person tells us, "The Lord says you're having trouble with someone at work, but the situation is not what you think.

Go talk to them about how He loves them, and you will see the situation change." That kind of prophetic word doesn't need multiple confirmations. The Bible talks about sharing God's love with other people, and we can just go do it.

> **Waiting for confirmation is one of the key ways we discern if a prophetic word is from God or from another source.**

But when someone gives us a prophetic word about a *major* direction change, an unexpected life shift, or something big that is going to affect other people, we need to wait for confirmation. Waiting for confirmation is one of the key ways we discern if a prophetic word is from God or from another source. Sometimes the "other source" isn't necessarily bad, but perhaps the word is just not meant for us.[5]

As we wait for confirmation, we will hear more from the Lord for ourselves. Eventually, if the word ends up being from Him, we will be able to respond to Him personally, not just because somebody lobbed an idea at us.

## 7. Does the Prophetic Word Contradict Something God Has Already Told Us?

Remember the young man from 1 Kings 13. God clearly told him not to stop to eat or drink, but the older prophet gave him a "word" saying the opposite. God will not contradict Himself. In the Sermon on the Mount, Jesus told us that our "yes" and "no" should be binding (see Matthew 5:37 and James 5:12). He is not going to say yes and no about the same thing! If we have

---

[5] *One example of this is when a person prophesies about something they need to do. They are feeling convicted over something, or the Lord is telling them to do something, but they haven't recognized it yet—so they are starting to prophesy it over everybody else. That can happen.*

heard something from God and have taken the time to discern it really is from Him, if someone gives us a "prophetic word" that says the opposite, we can throw it out.

God is having an ongoing conversation with us, and one prophetic experience is not the whole message. One prophetic encounter shouldn't be taken in isolation from all the other things God is doing in our life and speaking to us.[6]

Those are some helpful steps for discerning a prophetic word. In the next chapter, we will look at *soulish prophecies*, which take a bit more discernment to figure out.

---

[6] *We will explore this more in chapter 5: "Recognizing the Broader Conversation."*

# CHAPTER 3

## UNDERSTANDING SOULISH PROPHECIES

# UNDERSTANDING SOULISH PROPHECIES

A few years ago, I prophesied to someone about a change of season. A shift was about to happen in this person's life, and some new things were going to start.

The person went back and told their pastor, "John Thomas prophesied to me that I am going to leave my job."

That was not what I said! All I said was, "There is a change of season." I didn't know if it was related to their work, and I definitely did not tell them to leave their job. Yet that is what the person "heard" because that is what they wanted to hear. They didn't like their job and wanted out of that situation, so they grabbed on to the prophetic word and heard something I did not actually say.

This happens all the time in the prophetic community. The soul is comprised of what we think, want, and feel. It is a gift from God and can be a beautiful thing, but there are times when it is completely wrong! The soul is where we can make human assumptions and come to human conclusions based on our own strength.

Let's say someone gives you a prophetic word that doesn't violate Scripture or God's nature. It seems like it fits your life, and you can see how it *might* be from the Lord. Does that mean the word is from Him? Sometimes, but not always. Some "prophetic words" don't violate the Bible or what God says about Himself. In fact, the word might pass all the tests we talked about in the last chapter, but that doesn't mean the word is from God. Whenever the soul is involved, things can get messy.

There are three basic kinds of soulish prophecies:[7]

1.  Someone gives us a prophetic word, and our soul takes hold of it and convinces us God is saying something He is not saying.
2.  A prophetic individual gives us a word from their soul, not from the Holy Spirit.
3.  A prophetic individual senses what our soul is saying and speaks it back to us as "prophecy."

We will look at each of these soulish prophecies in turn, but first let's take a closer look at what the soul really is.

## What Is the Human Soul?

The Bible says we are made of three parts: spirit, soul, and body.

---

[7] *If this topic intrigues you, you may want to check out Streams Academy Phase 1: Prophetic and Revelatory Training. Module 2 explores this topic in greater depth.*

*Now may the God of peace Himself sanctify you completely, and may your whole spirit and soul and body be kept blameless at the coming of our Lord Jesus Christ. (1 Thessalonians 5:23)*

*For the word of God is living and active, sharper than any two-edged sword, piercing to the division of soul and of spirit, of joints and of marrow, and discerning the thoughts and intentions of the heart. (Hebrews 4:12)*

Before we meet the Lord, our spirit is dormant. It is shriveled up and asleep, and it is unable to interact with Him. When *His* Spirit comes and wakes us up, our spirit comes alive and begins to grow.

Like everything else in creation, the human spirit starts out immature. We are babies "in the spirit," and we need to grow up the same way a child needs to grow up, which takes time. In addition to time, we grow by responding to God's Spirit. The more we

grow up in Him, the more our spirit learns to rule over our soul. Our thoughts and desires begin to look more like our heavenly Father's thoughts and desires, because our spirit is ruling us.[8]

> **The more we grow up in Him, the more our spirit learns to rule over our soul.**

Historically, Christians have described the soul as the mind, will, and emotions, and this concept has been a part of the Church for a long time. From Augustine in the fourth century to Thomas Aquinas in the thirteenth century and beyond, the Body of Christ has talked about the soul being those three

---

[8] *John Paul Jackson develops this concept further in* The Art of Hearing God *course found in the streamsministries.com online classroom.*

things: the mind, the will, and the emotions. The Greek and Hebrew words for "soul" include those ideas. Hebrews 4:12 *divides* the soul and spirit, clearly delineating between them, and talks about God's Word judging the thoughts and intents of the heart. That is essentially the root of what the soul is: the thoughts and intents of the human heart.

When the spirit rules the soul, this is what the Bible refers to as being "Spirit led." But until that happens, the soul likes to pretend to be the spirit. "Oh, I know what God wants. I know what is best for me. I know exactly what we should do here! And we should probably do it as soon as possible."

A person's soul can affect revelation in various ways:

It can affect how we discern the revelation we receive. That is what happened in the story I told at the beginning of this chapter, where the person thought I said something I didn't say.

It can affect the way we receive revelation (or what we think is revelation).

The soul can also broadcast information other prophetic people can sense.

Here are a few clues that can help us discern when our soul is trying to rule us.

## The Soul Can Filter a Prophetic Word

The soul can filter what we hear from prophetic people and push us to interpret the prophecy according to the soul's desires. The soul can also influence our capacity to discern whether or not something is really from God. If we strongly desire something to happen, our discernment can run into a wall, and we might have trouble telling if a word is from God. The spirit needs to confirm His voice, not the soul. When He speaks, our spirit recognizes Him and cries, "Yes! I want this!" He confirms the word within us.

However, when we don't know the difference

between the soul and spirit, the soul can step into that place of ruling, and things can get a bit "sticky" when someone gives us a prophetic word. We have a hard time hearing what the spirit is saying, and the soul is right there to give confirmation:

- "Yes! This is what I've always wanted, and it's finally coming true!"
- "I've always felt this way. I've always thought this was true—and look, I was totally right."
- "This feels really good, so it must be God."

We feel a response and assume it is discernment, when it is simply our soul responding to an idea.

The solution to the spirit-soul conundrum is to constantly take what we think, what we feel, and what we want to God for His input. This is one of my favorite Bill Johnson quotes: "I can't afford to have a thought in my head about me that God does not have about me." In our context here, this means we need to take "captive" every thought, feeling, and desire we have and bring these things before the Lord, asking for His feedback and direction. What is He thinking? What does He want? What is He saying about our desires?

As we do this, we allow Him to change what needs changing. We give Him permission to mold us according to *His* wishes and desires (Philippians 2:13) and to bring us into agreement with His Word. In that place, we are much better able to discern what He is saying and know how to respond to it.

Jesus had to go through this spirit-soul process. His soul was overwhelmed and wanted to find a way out of the cross, but He was able to recognize it was His soul and bring it into submission to God's will. He gives us a key that helps us overcome the soul's attempt to rule the spirit: prayer.

*Then He said to them, "My soul is very sorrowful, even to death; remain here, and watch with Me." And going a little farther He fell on His face and prayed, saying, "My Father, if it be possible, let this cup pass from Me; nevertheless, not as I will, but as You will." And He came to the disciples and found them sleeping. And He said to Peter, "So, could you not watch with Me one hour? Watch and pray that you may not enter into temptation. The spirit indeed is willing, but the flesh is weak." (Matthew 26:38–41)*

The soul, our flesh, is weak. The spirit united with God's Spirit is willing. We have to choose the spirit and learn to recognize when our soul desires something other than God's will.

This internal "checking in" with God can become a habit in our life, and as it does, we become *steadier* in our walk with Him. We mature and can recognize His voice when we hear it—and also when we have not heard it.

## A Prophetic Person Can Sense What the Soul Wants

Humans have a natural capacity to recognize what is going on in other people's souls. A mother, for example, is often keenly aware of what her baby wants. "She's hungry. Her stomach hurts. Her feet hurt. She wants the toy." This connection gives the baby a sense of security, even though the child hasn't learned to communicate with words.

> **Humans have a natural capacity to recognize what is going on in other people's souls.**

As we develop relationships with other people, we naturally begin to pick up on what they are feeling, thinking, and wanting.

Only 30 or 40 percent of communication is words; another percentage is the person's intonation, followed by body language.

However, communication also happens within a person's *atmosphere*. We can sense what the person's soul is saying. Have you ever walked into a room and sensed someone was angry or hurt, even before you interacted with the person? This can happen because the soul is broadcasting emotions.

There is nothing wrong with the soul communicating this way. It is very natural. However, if we allow the soul with its human thoughts and desires to grow unchecked, these things could become hard and stubborn and shift into what the Bible calls a stronghold: a set pattern of thinking, feeling, or wanting.

As the name suggests, a stronghold is formidable. The more powerful the stronghold, the more we start to fight for and argue about what we think, want, and feel. Eventually we stop allowing God or others to speak to us—unless their input agrees with what we already think or want. Strongholds are one of the root causes of misunderstanding words from God.

A stronghold can gradually grow into an idol in our heart. We start to believe that certain ideas and desires *almost* equate with God's ideas and desires. We might not say it that way, but it is true for us emotionally. We check in with those things before we obey the Lord. They become our greatest pursuit, and the totality of our life starts to move in their direction. Anything can become a stronghold and then an idol. For some people, it is their education. For others, it is success, gifting, or ministry. An idol is anything other than God that holds the focus of our life.

Keep in mind that when something becomes a stronghold, and later an idol, this does not automatically mean that thing is evil. It just means we have put too much importance on it. If God has called us to make wealth so we can build His kingdom, it is good to desire more understanding about business strategies and different ways to grow wealth. If He has called us to get married and have a family, it is good to desire to meet the right person and marry them. If He has called us to a specific ministry, it is good to desire to be in that ministry.

Every time we know the calling of God, it is good to desire that calling and pursue it. However, the calling itself cannot become our goal. The goal of our life needs to be the Lord. If it is anything other than Him, we are following an idol. To read more on this subject, spend some time in Ezekiel 14, where God talked about speaking to people *according to the idol*. The idol was what they heard, which was not a good thing.

Strongholds speak more loudly than other parts of the soul. If a stronghold is allowed to flourish, it slowly becomes a "house" that demonic entities can influence to the point of producing revelation. It is not real revelation, of course; it is not from God, but it broadcasts information out into the atmosphere, and other people can sometimes hear it and mistakenly assume they are hearing the Lord for that person.

Anyone who has developed their capacity to hear prophetically will be able to sense what a person's soul is saying. Unfortunately, even in the prophetic movement, many people don't realize this is happening. They just assume they are hearing from God, and so they turn around and prophesy the information as if it were from Him. It is true they are picking up on something they had no previous knowledge of, but the "revelation" is a mirror image of what the person was already thinking, wanting, or feeling. It fits their soul because it originated from their soul.

When someone gives us a prophetic word that feels strongly familiar, like something we have already thought about or deeply desired, we need to take extra time to discern it. We shouldn't automatically dismiss it, but neither should we automatically assume it is from God, because it *could* be from our soul.

> **Anyone who has developed their capacity to hear prophetically will be able to sense what a person's soul is saying.**

The more we mature in hearing God, the more we learn to recognize when other people are reading our soul, so we don't take what they say as if it were a promise from Him. Instead, we take it with a grain of salt and ask the Lord about it. "God, You know this is something I have wanted for a very long time. Is this what You are really saying to me?"

## A Prophetic Person Can Sense the Human Spirit

If a prophetic person can sense the desires of our soul, they might also sense the desires of our spirit. There are times when our spirit—the special part of us that is joined with the Holy Spirit (1 Corinthians 6:17)—is crying out for something from the Lord. "Lord, please come and do this thing! Move on my behalf. Open this door. Fulfill this promise."

These kinds of prayers are holy and sacred. If a prophetic person picks up on one of these prayers, hopefully they recognize it as a prayer and say so. The prophetic word needs to be communicated this way: "Your heart is crying out for this." Or "I can feel the prayer coming out of your spirit for such-and-such to happen." There are times, however, when a prophetic person assumes the prayer is a promise of what God is just about to do. They might say, "God says He's just about to do this in your life. This is just around the corner." That could be true, but it isn't exactly what the Lord is saying.

When someone gives us a prophetic word that matches one of the deep prayers in our spirit, we are responsible for responding to it appropriately. Again, we take the word before the Lord and ask Him about it. "Lord, I've been praying about this for a long time. Is this what You are really saying? *Are* You just about to do this? Is this the right time?"

## Knowing Yourself and His Word

In the fourth century, Augustine prayed this prayer: "Lord, teach me to know myself, so that I may know You." The better we know ourselves, the more we will be able to recognize what is God, what is us, where the two merge, and where they separate. When we know ourselves, we have a much better understanding of what is soul and what is spirit. We know what is going on in our own mind, heart, and will, so we can recognize when a prophetic word fits what we already think, want, and feel. The word could very well be from the Lord, but we will need to spend more time discerning if it is from Him or if it is just a reflection of our desire.

In the garden the night before He was crucified, Jesus prayed, "I really don't want to do this, but if You want it, I will do it." We can use that same basic prayer when we speak to God about a prophecy we received: "I really want to do this, but if You don't want me to, I am willing to say no. I want to submit every part of me to You and what You have for me. What do You say about this? What are Your thoughts?"

When that is our mindset, we are better able to recognize when the word is really from God. Then, when we know a prophetic word is from the Lord, we can take the next step. "This is You, isn't it? This is what You are saying to me. What do I do with this prophetic word? How do You want me to proceed?"

Knowing ourselves is important, and so is knowing Scripture. Hebrews 4:12 says the

Word of God is like a sword that divides the soul from the spirit. As we spend time reading Scripture, studying it, and meditating on it, our ability to recognize the difference between our soul and spirit grows. We become more sensitive to the ways of God, and when something doesn't align with His ways, it just feels wrong. Truth becomes a plumb line that tests everything around us, and when our soul rises up and speaks, we recognize, "I really want this, but this specific thing right now is not the will of God." Our ability to discern revelation directly correlates with our knowledge of Scripture, our alignment with it, and our time with Him.

**Truth becomes a plumb line that tests everything around us.**

In the next chapter, we will talk about how certain prophetic words—especially those that are about a major life change—often need to be taken to spiritual leaders in our life, so we can receive their counsel and understand what to do next.

# CHAPTER 4

## RELYING ON LEADERS TO HELP YOU DISCERN PROPHETIC WORDS

# RELYING ON LEADERS TO HELP YOU DISCERN PROPHETIC WORDS

Several years ago, Dawna and I were part of an amazing church that faithfully and lovingly discipled us. God used this church to help us grow, and certain foundations we learned there are still an active part of who we are today.

Eventually, however, we reached a point where both of us knew that to continue growing in what God had for us, we needed to go somewhere else. A phrase from John Wimber haunted us: "The things of the kingdom are more caught than taught."

There was more of God than what we were experiencing, and we needed to be around it if we wanted to "catch" what He had planned for us.

At the time, God was talking to us about fivefold ministry and how it operates. We wanted to know more about the apostolic and prophetic, which we felt would be a key part of what He had for us. As we sensed His call, Dawna and I began praying and asking Him what He wanted us to do.

One day I saw an announcement from MorningStar Ministries about their new ministry school. I dearly loved MorningStar; they had woken me up in a season when I was starting to fall asleep as a believer. Listening to their worship had caused something in my heart to come alive and had quickened my spirit. Some of the wisdom I gleaned from Rick Joyner just astounded me, especially his book *Shadows of Things to Come*. Their ad about the school mentioned teaching people about fivefold ministry, including the apostolic and prophetic, which was exactly what Dawna and I wanted.

*This is it,* I thought. *This is where we're supposed to go.*

Dawna and I prayed about it, and we both agreed this was a good step for us. We started looking for property down in North Carolina so we could build a house. We found something we liked, talked to people about it, and prepped a floor plan. We were ready.

However, knowing how important it is to work with leaders, we decided to sit down with our pastor, explain the situation, and see what he thought. Dawna and I told him, "This is where we are. This is what we feel we're supposed to do and how we have been led so far."

To our surprise, our pastor replied, "You know what? I have some concerns about their teaching—specifically what they teach about the fivefold. I don't really agree with everything they teach. I don't think this is God, and I don't think this is a good idea."

We wanted to go to MorningStar *because* their teaching about fivefold ministry was different than our pastor's, and that was his concern. He did not give us his blessing, and we wanted his blessing.

And so, we decided to wait. Dawna and I canceled our plans and went back to the drawing board, praying, "God, please show us what is going on." We chose to see the situation through the lens of Proverbs 21:1: "The king's heart is a stream of water in the hand of the Lord; He turns it wherever He will." We trusted God was in this unexpected change, even though we didn't like it.

Over the next several months, we continued to pray, and we felt God speaking to us. The revelation grew clearer, and we realized

He actually wanted us to move up to New Hampshire to be a part of Streams Ministries and help out John Paul Jackson.

> **We trusted God was in this unexpected change, even though we didn't like it.**

Again, we scheduled a meeting with our pastor, sat down with him, and began to explain, "Here's what's going on. This is what we believe God is saying, and this is what we're thinking."

And again, he expressed some of the same thoughts he had the first time. "You know, I have concerns with some of the things John Paul Jackson teaches, especially about the apostolic and the prophetic." Then he added, "But I think this is God. Let me know when your last Sunday is here. I want to lay hands on you and bless you guys as you go out."

We received our blessing.

I learned a valuable lesson through all of this. I thought Dawna and I had heard God clearly. Part of me complained, "We are supposed to go to the MorningStar ministry school, and our pastor is keeping us from God's will!"

But as I was grumbling and arguing with Him about why He would give us a leader who didn't allow us to go after what He wanted, I was mistaken—and our pastor was right. I had not heard God clearly. Our pastor discerned what we could not discern, and God used him to hold us in place until we could hear what He was really saying. As a result, we went to Streams and started down a wonderful path that led us to this book you're reading. Many of my accomplishments in life would not exist if we hadn't submitted to our leader and allowed him to help us discern revelation.

## All of Us Need Wise Leaders

When someone gives us a prophetic word about a big life change, or we feel like God is speaking directly to us about one, we can take that word to wise leaders and see what they think. As Proverbs 11:14 says, "Where there is no guidance, a people falls, but in an abundance of counselors there is safety." The word *counselors* appears several times in Proverbs, and it is because we need them. A multitude of counselors keeps us safe in times of war and helps us see what we have trouble seeing. When wise people speak into us, the result is many blessings.

In the United States, we tend to think

independently. "I don't need anybody. I can hear God for myself." Some of that is true; we always need to seek God for ourselves and learn how to hear His voice. At the same time, He did not create us, or the world around us, to operate in isolation. If we will listen to the voices He has set in place for us and be willing to submit ourselves to what He is saying through them, we will find greater success. We need to learn how to work with pastors, advisors, mentors, and the other people God has brought into our life.

When the Lord invited you and me to follow Him, He invited us into a family—a community He is building that represents Him to the world. Within that community, He anoints leaders to help us. They can see our part in the story He is telling and can help us accomplish the purpose He put us here to accomplish.

All of us need to learn how to talk about

prophetic words with our leaders. One of the first steps in this process is learning how to trust God inside those leaders. Proverbs 21:1 is a valuable truth that is often more active in our life than we realize: God can turn the hearts of kings (the men and women He has put in our life to help guide us) like He turns water. He can move them this way, or He can move them that way. When we are fully confident in God's ability to shift the hearts of kings, we will be able to receive great counsel from them—even if they don't realize what is going on.

**What Do Wise Leaders Look Like?**

Wise counselors are men and women who know doctrine and Scripture better than we do. They have walked with God longer than we have and display the fruit of faithfulness in their lives. When they give us feedback, we recognize, "Wait a second. This is the Lord speaking to me through this person. I thought this prophetic word was from God, but now I can see it doesn't look like His heart."

> **People who know God's heart and nature can help us discern His heart and nature.**

People who know God's heart and nature can help us discern His heart and nature. Here are a few simple things we can look for when trying to recognize the leaders in our life:

- They are people full of God's love. His love moves through them easily.
- They follow the Holy Spirit and live according to the Spirit's fruit, practicing gentleness, self-control, patience, etc.

- They are spirit ruled, not soul ruled. They are concerned with God's wishes and desires and aren't carnally minded.[9]
- They have a track record of hearing from God accurately. (They don't have to be 100 percent perfect in this regard, but their general track record is good and trustworthy.)
- They have been walking with God for a long time. They are not new to following the Spirit and are not new believers.

People who operate in spiritual wisdom can say, "Well, if this is what God is saying and doing in your life, this is probably how you should respond." They have life experience with following His leading and can step in to help us move forward. They are not merely educated, but they are sincerely mature in their faith.

---

[9] *Sometimes the people who are closest to you should not be where you go for wisdom about discerning prophetic words. If your close friends or family don't have spiritual maturity, they can end up giving you human wisdom, not what the Spirit of God is saying.*

The goal of spiritual counsel is to discern God's will, not just to have someone tell us what we are hoping to hear. Therefore, if we want to grow, we need to seek out the truth tellers, not the "yes men." Truth tellers tell the truth because they care about us enough to challenge us if necessary. These people are a gold mine and can help us discern what is God and what is not, what He sounds like, what His heart for us is like, etc.

Solid spiritual leaders in our life know us well and can help us discern when something might be our soul. "You have talked about doing this for years. This is something you really, really want. How did this revelation come to you? Are you sure it was God, or is it possible this is your soul expressing a desire?" These are not difficult or controlling questions. They are asked in love and can help us discern God's voice and grow in His wisdom.

In the past, the Church relied on people called spiritual directors: men and women who were spiritually mature and knew God's voice well. They would help other people discern His voice and their revelatory experiences and recognize how to go deeper in the things of the Spirit. Some of these spiritual directors left behind writings that are still full of wisdom and revelation today. This is where we get books like *The Imitation of Christ* by Thomas á Kempis, *Interior Castles* by St. Teresa of Avila, *The Dark Night of the Soul* by St. John of the Cross, and *Experiencing the Depths of Jesus Christ* by Madame Guyon. Each of these writers was a spiritual director who helped people discern Him and what He was doing.

We all need spiritual directors today: people we can talk to about our faith and share our sins and struggles with. Humble leaders who will listen to us, who will tell us about God's forgiveness, who will advise us and keep us accountable—not just in the avoidance of sin but in the pursuit of our dreams and the remarkable vision God gave us for our life. People who will remind us of His word over our life and show us how things fit into that word.

Spiritual directors help us discern revelation and respond to God accordingly.

## When Do We Need to Seek Counsel?

A prophetic word about a life change or a radically different season requires more time to discern. Especially in these cases, we need spiritual directors in our life.

"Small" prophetic words like "God wants you to be a light for Him at work" or "Practice being more generous with strangers" have little to no cost to them. They don't require much time to discern. But when the word is big, we always need to go to the spiritually mature people God has put into our life and get them involved in our discerning process. This opens the door to wise counsel that keeps us safe and guides us into God's plan. We will be able to avoid traps of self-deception, which are pretty easy to stumble into when no one is there to catch us. All of us fall into those traps at some time or another, which is why we need each other so much.

Many people are afraid of the prophetic because of the mistakes that occurred in the past. These fears become almost nonexistent when a person has wise leaders they are willing to listen to.

# CHAPTER 5

# RECOGNIZING THE BROADER CONVERSATION

# RECOGNIZING THE BROADER CONVERSATION

Dawna and I lived in New England for years. Eventually we stepped away from Streams to lead a church in Massachusetts, but about five years later, we began to feel the Holy Spirit leading us to work with Streams again, which had since moved down to Texas.

When we realized what God was saying to us, I picked up my dream journal and started looking through it, specifically at my dreams from the last twelve to eighteen months. Remarkably, I found a number of dreams I thought I had understood at the time—and perhaps they did have an application back then—but they *also* had an application for now, as we prepared to move south.

Also, I had never been able to figure out certain dreams. I could tell they were from the Lord, but I couldn't put my finger on what they meant. All at once, they began to make sense. They were talking about my new role at Streams and what it would look like. In fact, some dreams actually prophesied that one day I would lead Streams, but I couldn't see that piece until after John Paul Jackson, the Streams founder, had passed away.

There was a lot to think about as we prepared to move to Texas, and I started having little "daydreams" about what I would do in certain situations. What would I do if XYZ happened? How would I respond? I thought I was just processing or maybe learning some things, but after I became the president of Streams, I remembered those "daydreams" and realized some of them were God giving me strategies for the future. He was showing me what to do before I ever stepped into those situations.

This sometimes surprising "blending" of events, dreams, thoughts, and prophecy happens because our conversation with the Lord is ongoing. It doesn't start and stop or have random, unconnected pieces. Our relationship with Him isn't multiple books sitting together on a shelf; it is one book with many chapters, and all of them are connected.

> **The prophetic words you receive are just one part of your broader conversation with God.**

The prophetic words you receive are just one part of your broader conversation with God. What are you thinking and dreaming about? What is God highlighting to you in Scripture? What sticks out to you and grabs your attention? What has God been doing in your life? What miracles have you experienced? What doors have opened (or closed)? How do these things fit together with the word you received?

Every time you get a prophetic word, take some time to discern how the word fits into your ongoing conversation with the Lord.

## We Prophesy "in Part"

A prophetic word is a glimpse of what God is doing. It is not the whole picture. The Bible says we see in part and prophesy in part (1 Corinthians 13:9). Any prophetic word we receive—including one from an established prophetic voice we trust—is likely just one piece of what God is saying. When we put the different pieces together, we start to see a bigger, clearer picture.

Other than the church elders, Dawna and

I didn't immediately tell anyone we were moving to Texas. We wanted to share the news with our church at the right time. However, one Sunday morning when I was preaching, God started talking to one of the church members, and He took me by surprise.

When the sermon ended, I opened the service up for Q&A.

One of our church intercessors asked, "John, what do cowboy boots mean?" *Well, this is an interesting question*, I thought. *It doesn't have anything to do with the service, but I'll go with it.* "What is the context? Things have meaning in context."

She replied, "The whole time you've been preaching this morning, you've been wearing cowboy boots in the spirit. I'm just wondering what cowboy boots mean."

I nearly lost it—God was telling my secrets!

I didn't share with her the full meaning right then, but once the information became public, I had a conversation with her. "Remember when you asked me about cowboy boots and what they meant? This move is what that picture was talking about."

Her "piece" was one sentence in an ongoing conversation I was having with the Lord. The cowboy boots made sense in the overall context of that conversation, even though the image didn't make much sense on its own.

When God gives us a word, it is not separate from the rest of our conversation with Him. We will have an easier time responding to a prophetic word when we understand what He is saying in the *whole conversation*, not just the word itself. All of us prophesy in part, and the more pieces we have, the greater the opportunity to perceive His words clearly.

Let's say a prophetic individual tells us,

"You're going to have great influence." Okay, but that could mean so many different things:

- What kind of influence?
- Influence with whom?
- Is it great influence on *one* person? Or is it great influence because it will affect *many* people?
- Is it influence in the religious arena? In the political arena? In the economic arena?
- Do we need to position ourselves for the influence, or is it just going to happen?

We won't know what God means if we focus on the word by itself: "You're going to have great influence." This is where our broader conversation with Him comes into play. When He speaks, He is adding to the lifelong conversation we are already having with Him. Therefore, we can look at what else He has said to us and—in many cases—be able to recognize how the new prophetic word fits into the bigger picture.

Whether we realize it or not, whether we understand it or not, God has been speaking to us from before we were born. Everything we have gone through—the good, the bad, the ugly, the beautiful—is an experience that can help us discern what He is saying today, as well as how and when we need to respond to His words.

Here are a few things that can help us recognize the long, detailed conversation we are having with God:

- What have we learned? How were we educated? (Not necessarily schooling, but the lessons and principles we learned through experience.)
- How are we gifted?
- Where are we capable?
- What is already in our hands? A couple of times in Scripture, God asked different people, "What is in your hand?" He sometimes uses what we already have to help us accomplish what is coming next.

- What are we passionate about?

- What moves our heart—good or bad? Sometimes we can recognize a calling by what annoys us. If we hate it every time we hear about injustice, perhaps we are called to fight for justice. If deception bugs us, perhaps we are called to fight for truth.

- What kinds of people are around us? What kinds of opportunities do we have? What kinds of opportunities do we *not* have?

As we look at the broad picture of our life, we can add the revelation we have received into that picture and begin to see more clearly what God is saying and doing. Decision-making becomes much easier when we know the broader conversation. It is like God whispers to our spirit, "This really is what I am saying. You are hearing Me correctly. Do you see how this new prophetic word fits in with the others?"

> **Decision-making becomes much easier when we know the broader conversation.**

Here at Streams, we stress the importance of writing down dreams, and that is one reason it is so important—they are part of our broader conversation with God. As we recognize He is guiding us into something new, it is incredibly helpful to look through our dreams and see what they add to our conversation with Him.

- Do any of these dreams reflect the new thing God is doing?
- Are there any themes that "go with" the decision we need to make?

Not every dream will be about the decision we need to make, of course, but we may find that God has been talking to us about it for months. This is common.

We can do the same thing with all revelation we receive—prophetic words from other people, Scriptures the Holy Spirit highlights to us, encounters we have, things we wrote down in faith in our prayer journal, etc. We can also look at the prayers we have been praying. What is on our heart? What really matters to us in this season? What have we been asking God for? What has He already told us? Also, what have we been discussing with other people? Is there a theme to our conversations—a topic that keeps coming up? All these things play a role in the special, broader conversation we are having with God, and they can help us see how a new prophetic word fits into our walk with Him.

## Even the Little Things Mean Something

When we find the bigger picture, we find

greater faith. The more pieces we have, the more we have to work with and the clearer the picture will be. The little pieces add up over time, and they increase our confidence about what God is saying.

Going back to the simple prophetic word about "great influence," here's how the little things can work together to reveal the big things:

- Someone prays for us and gives us the word about having great influence.
- A few weeks later, somebody at work randomly mentions we have a teaching gift. "You're just really good at talking to other people and helping them understand what's going on."
- A prophetic friend tells us how God is about to show us secrets in Scripture that will help other people. "It's important for you to record what God is saying to you."
- Another prophetic individual starts talking about how we have "a voice."

- One night we have a dream where a huge number of people are listening to us, and they all want to know what God is saying.

We are thinking and praying about what all of this could mean—and then one day we realize God might be talking to us about starting a podcast, where we take the truths we are finding in Scripture, record them, and make them available to a broad spectrum of people. God is going to use our voice and the things we have learned in Scripture to bring about great influence in this arena.

All the individual pieces might seem small in the moment, but they add up like coins, and eventually we have a treasure of great worth. God doesn't start and end a conversation with one prophetic word. A prophetic word is just one sentence. As we realize how that one sentence fits into the broader conversation, we start to understand how we need to respond—and *when* we need to respond.

## Bigger Decisions, More Revelation

If we are facing a big decision, and God has talked to us only once about it, it is possible the timing isn't right. Maybe we have the "what," but we don't have the "when." We need both in order to obey what God is saying.

Many people worry about prophecy and feel pressure to move quickly, but the Lord won't hold us responsible for something we don't know. There is no reason for us to worry about "missing it" with Him, because He will give us what we need at the right time as long as our heart is willing. We can trust He will supply the other pieces and everything will be in order.

> **The Lord won't hold us responsible for something we don't know.**

If we don't have the whole picture yet, all we need to do is keep our eyes open and pay attention to anything He says. Once we know what we are supposed to do, we obey, but if all we know is that something is going to happen, we wait. Maybe we know we will go to other nations one day, but we don't know which ones or how God is going to use us there. So we wait until He clarifies. Sometimes God speaks very clearly the first time—think of Abraham being told to sacrifice Isaac or Joseph being told to take Mary and Jesus to Egypt. But often the word is not clear at the beginning, and we need to wait until we have a better understanding of what He is saying.

## Recognizing Themes

A few years ago, someone gave me a prophetic word about doing live videos. They said, "Live is going to be important. It's the most important word right now."

Because of that simple prophecy, we began

a deeper exploration of social media and figured out how to use Facebook Live. We started doing live online teachings and saw a small amount of fruit from them.

Some time after this, I realized I needed to start using Zoom. "I need to understand how this works. Zoom is an important thing for Streams to be able to do." It was just an impression, but I felt it was significant. So we bought the different equipment we needed, even though we didn't really know why we needed it, and started playing around with it.

As I spoke with people, I began to get this idea of doing virtual conferences. What if, instead of people coming together physically, we brought them together online? What would that look like? How would it work? Was it possible we could use Zoom, and if so, how would we set it up? I wasn't sure how to go about doing a conference that was entirely online, and I was traveling so much I didn't have time to figure it out. But it seemed like an interesting idea.

Then covid hit. The world screeched to a halt. My travel schedule cleared, and I realized how God had prepared Streams for that moment. It began with a prophetic word, followed by an idea for doing things online. In the beginning, the gumption wasn't there—that internal weight of the Spirit that helps us know when the timing is right. But the timing *became* right. We didn't know what we were preparing for, but God did. All these things came together at the right time. We recognized what He was saying, and we were able to step into the virtual conference world without delay, because He had prepared us.

Finding these themes—the special connections between personal revelation, prophetic words, and timing—is so much fun! As we find them, we become more confident about what God is saying, and knowing what to do next becomes easier.

## Embracing the Mystery of How God Speaks

When the Lord speaks, He usually doesn't explain how the prophecy will come about. Again and again in Scripture, we find stories where He told people to do nearly impossible things, and He didn't tell them *how*.

One example of this principle is Gideon. At the beginning of his story, Gideon was scared and trying to hide, and nobody paid attention to him. No one even knew his name. But God told him, "You are going to save My people." Because of that revelation, Gideon ended up becoming the leader of his nation. Other revelations helped get him there, but not once did God tell him how things were going to work out. Gideon knew only what he was supposed to do and when he was supposed to do it, and then—when he did what God said—somehow everything worked. That is often how a word from the Lord comes about.

If we wait until we understand how a prophetic word will happen, we lose the mystery and the potential for miracles. Many times we end up doing nothing, and God has to move without us. Trying to know everything in advance can lead to missing out on the great stories we love to tell each other about God's creativity in our life and how He did astounding things.

John Paul Jackson used to say, "You don't need a miracle until you need a miracle!" When we allow ourselves to step into what God has said, even when what He said doesn't make sense—that is when we begin to see the miraculous.

# CHAPTER 6

## WHAT DO I DO NOW?

# WHAT DO I DO NOW?

Here are three of the most common types of revelation and how to respond to them. Abraham experienced all three types: God gave him identity revelation in Genesis 15:5–6 ("Your descendants will be as numerous as the stars"). He received a correction word in Genesis 21:12 ("Do what your wife says") and direction revelation in Genesis 22:1–2 (sacrificing Isaac).

**Identity Revelation**

Many, many times when God speaks to us, He addresses who we are.

- "You are loved."
- "You are able to do this thing."

- "You are capable."
- "I have given you the capacity to succeed where others have failed."
- "You are forgiven."
- "You are My treasure."
- "You are My beloved child."

Those are all issues of identity—truths about who we really are. When God speaks about our identity, our first response is to believe Him, because He cannot lie. If He says something is true about us, we can relax and believe it, because it is true. He is the only One who really does know who we are, and He has no level of deception within Himself. We can bank on what He is saying with all our heart.

Our second response to identity revelation is to pray about the revelation until it becomes part of our heart. We can tell our mind to agree with God, but that doesn't mean the revelation will drop down into our heart. We actually need God to move—to take what is in our mind and bring it down to our heart, which happens through the blessed interaction of prayer.

> **Pray about the revelation until it becomes part of our heart.**

The process is similar to a very short prayer found in the book of Mark. A desperate father brought his demon-possessed son to Jesus and the disciples, hoping to find freedom for the boy.

Jesus said, "If you have faith, anything is possible."

The dad reacted, essentially crying out, "I do believe! Help my unbelief. I want to believe what You are saying."

We can pray the same way. "Father, I know You are saying this about me, and I want to believe it." We "pray in" the revelation God has given us.

The next step is declaring the revelation over ourselves. "This is who I am. This is what the Word says about me. This is what God says about me."

I can't tell you how many prophetic words I have received telling me I am God's beloved. Obviously, that is true for all His children, but every time I hear this word from someone, it is special to me. I have been declaring it over myself for years now: "I am beloved of the Father. I know there is a special place in His heart for me." When I am having a hard time remembering who I am, when I feel scared or incapable, I speak that revelation over myself. I hold on to it and declare it. That is a good way to respond whenever someone gives us a prophetic word having to do with our identity.

**Correction Words**

A correction word is when God wants to fix an ungodly attitude or behavior we have adopted. Our first response to a correction word is, obviously, to receive the correction.

Whenever the Lord corrects us, we can put the correction in the context of His nature—specifically, that He is good and kind toward us. Therefore, if He is correcting us, it is for our good. He doesn't correct us because He fears our sin, like other people sometimes do, but He corrects us because He loves us. He wants us to walk in the fullness of His love, which becomes much easier when we are willing to receive His correction.

One important part of receiving a correction word is repentance. We repent for the negative attitude or behavior God wants to correct. Then we acknowledge (confess) that what we were doing was wrong and get it out in the open. Whenever something remains hidden, the enemy has a level of authority in that place. We cut off his authority as we confess our sins to trustworthy sources like friends, family, our small group, etc.

Another important part of a correction word is finding healing. Why did we choose a sinful path? What was the reason behind our actions? We especially need inner healing when the issue is something God already addressed in the past, but we are still struggling with it. Did a painful event in our past mark us in some way? Did we make an inner vow? "I will never do this again!" or "I will *always* do this." Perhaps a generational issue needs to be dealt with—our parent or grandparent also struggled with some form of this exact issue. Or maybe we are reaping a judgment we made a long time ago: "All men will reject me," "All women will hurt me," etc. That "root" needs to be dug up. A variety of different things could be going on.[10]

---

[10] For more information on inner healing, I recommend a book called *Streams of Healing*. I wrote a chapter about how revelation connects with inner healing.

**Direction Words**

A direction word is when God tells us what to do. Direction words fall into two basic categories: *momentary* and *seasonal*. In most cases, a momentary direction word has one main action that is pretty easy to understand:

- "I want you to do this."
- "I want you to talk to your co-worker about Me."
- "Go pray for this person."
- "Go on that missions trip."

With a direction word, one of the first things we need to do is discern the cost involved. How much will it cost us to follow the word if it ends up *not* being from the Lord? We talked about this in an earlier chapter, but the higher the cost, the more revelation we need. Some momentary direction words don't carry a high price. If the word is "God wants you to go pray for your neighbor," there is not much cost involved. We check in with God and make sure that really is what He is saying, and when we know it is, all we need is simple obedience.[11] With many momentary direction words, even if it wasn't God telling us to go do that thing, there is no harm in doing it. If we are not sure if He is telling us to go pray for our neighbor, we can still pray for them. We don't need a prophetic word to do something that is already clear in Scripture!

Other direction words, however, have a substantial cost. Think of the rich young ruler in Scripture. Jesus told him to go sell everything he had and give the money to the poor. That was a big price to pay. If someone gives us a word about selling everything we own or picking up and moving to another country as a missionary, wisdom in that

---

[11] If God tells us to speak to someone or to pray for them, we need to be careful how we present the word to that person. If He told us just to pray for them, then we need to make sure that is all we do. Some prophetic individuals feel a need to make a simple word into something more extraordinary: "God told me He's going to heal you right now!" Did God actually say that? Or did He tell them just to pray? We need to communicate the words of the Lord in humility, and if we miss it, then we miss it—that is all. There is no greater risk than we look like we missed it. We don't need to add any "weight" to what He is saying.

situation looks like waiting for God to confirm the word first. This is especially true if we have a family we are responsible for. If God has called us to sell everything and move, He has also called our family, because they will be affected by the decision. Therefore, they need to be involved in the decision-making process. The word needs to be confirmed to them as well. The larger the life change, the more revelation we need.

> **The larger the life change, the more revelation we need.**

Also, certain direction words have a strong emphasis on timing. Especially when the cost is high, we need to discern when God wants us to do what He is calling us to do. I knew a man who received a word about leading a large ministry that would bring thousands of people to the Lord. Instead of seeking God for the timing, the man went out and tried to make the word happen on his own. He got a position with a ministry that did crusade evangelism, but he saw very little fruit. He became frustrated and decided, "That word must have been wrong." A few years later, he was asked to head up a discipleship ministry that led thousands to the Lord, just like the word said.

Sometimes there is a big difference between "Go do this" and "This is going to happen." When we take the time to get with the Lord and discern what He is saying to us, we become more sensitive to His leading, and we don't get ahead of Him.

A seasonal direction word is not momentary or brief, but it is a significant change or revelation about a person's life. Here are some examples:

- "You are called to be a doctor."

- "You're going to have a high position in your nation's government."
- "God has called you to lead intercessory groups around the world."

When God speaks this way, we need to seek Him for wisdom. Instead of trying to make the word happen, we prepare ourselves and get ready for *God* to move.

Think of it like surfing. We prepare by getting into the water with our surfboard, and then we wait until we see the wave we want. When we see it coming from a distance, we start paddling out to meet it—*before* it arrives, so we are already moving and can catch it more easily. The wave gives us momentum and propels us forward, and we are able to ride it. With a significant prophetic word, we can't make the wave appear, but when we see it coming from a distance, we can position our board, start paddling out to meet it, and get ready for it to carry us.

"Paddling out" to meet a prophetic wave can

look like different things. Even preparation takes discernment. When we know what the Lord is saying, we need to spend time with Him and ask Him pertinent questions. The questions might change based on the word and situation.

- "What do I need to develop now so I can step into this word when You fulfill it?"
- "Is there anything in me that would hinder the word or keep it from coming to pass?"
- "Does my mindset need to change? If so, *how* should it change?"
- "Do I need to work on anything?"
- "Do I need training or to develop certain skills?"

Developing our skills in advance is a common way to prepare for the future God has for us. At the same time, however, sometimes a direction word has *nothing* to do with skill. A friend of mine once had a dream about playing the drums, and around the same time, someone gave him a word about keeping rhythm. So my friend went out and bought himself a djembe. The following week at our small group, he was keeping rhythm with his new drum, and all of a sudden, he started singing prophetically. It is a difficult thing to play a drum and sing at the same time, but he was able to do it.

Unfortunately, there are a lot of stories about people who received prophetic words concerning worship, but they never learned how to play an instrument. The invitation was there, but they chose not to develop their skills. Just as it is possible to miss a prophetic word if we try to make it happen ourselves, it is also possible to miss a prophetic word if we don't prepare for it.

Let's say someone prophesies that we are going to be a missionary in Cambodia, working to bring healing and reformation in the prison system. We pray about the word, get feedback from leaders in our life, and come to realize the word is really from the Lord. Here are some important questions we can ask ourselves in advance:

- Is there anything in our life that might hinder the word? Are we deeply in debt? Are we struggling with character issues? It would be wise to take care of these things now, before the word starts to happen.
- Do we know the local language? If not, we need to find a teacher and learn it.
- Do we have a passport? Does it need to be renewed?
- What is the prison system like in Cambodia?

Or maybe we received a prophecy about owning a business. In advance of this word coming to pass, there are several important things we can ask ourselves and pray about:

- What kind of business is it? Will we require a certain skillset?
- What kind of training do we need?

- Are we going to create or engineer something? What do we need to learn in advance so our invention actually works?
- Are we going into the food industry? Do we know how to cook?
- Do we know how to start a business?
- Do we know anything about management?
- Do we know about inventory control and planning?

When we *know* we heard the Lord, we can start preparing for the word now, and then we will be ready when the time comes.

Many years ago, my life looked different than it does now. I was a teller at a bank. I knew the Lord was calling me to preach, but outside of a few small speaking invitations, the word had not yet come to pass. I started looking at my life, and I realized, "This prophetic word is going to be difficult with where I am right now. I need to prepare myself so when the word happens, I can step into it."

So I started preparing sermons and practicing my public speaking skills. The bank I worked in had a large boardroom in the back that no one used anymore. A conference table with a podium sat in the center of the room. On my lunch breaks, I would go into that room with my notes and my Bible, close the door, stand at the podium, and preach a message to an empty room. No one saw me or heard me, but I knew what God was saying—that one day I would preach. I wanted to develop my capacity and skillset so I would be ready when the time came.

We can't make a prophetic word happen, but we can do many things to prepare for what God has told us—like a surfer waiting for the perfect wave. When it comes, we can step right into it, and it is a beautiful thing.

## What If God Tells You Not to Prepare?

There are times when God talks about a person's future but doesn't want them to prepare for it. I have interpreted many dreams where He revealed something about the dreamer's future and didn't give them any instructions. In fact, the dream implied they didn't need to do anything at all.

With certain prophetic words, God wants us to wait and watch. *Not* preparing for a word takes just as much discernment as preparing for one.

If you have received such a word, take the word to your leaders and seek their counsel. Pray about the word, and regularly review everything the Lord has told you about it. Don't feel pressured to get out there and make the word happen. God knows what He is doing, and *He* can make the word happen at the right time.

# CHAPTER 7

# WHAT IF A PROPHETIC WORD TAKES A LONG TIME?

# WHAT IF A PROPHETIC WORD TAKES A LONG TIME?

Probably all of us know what it feels like to be given an exciting prophetic word that we can't wait to see happen—but nothing changes in our life. It is like the word stalls out. When a prophecy feels like it is taking forever, what can we do?

Here are a few suggestions that can comfort our heart and help us get ready—or stay ready—during the waiting time.

**Review the Revelation**

Take the time to refresh your heart in the

specific things God has spoken over you and your destiny, because this will give you life over the long haul. Especially when a promise seems delayed, it is a good idea to review the revelation.

Look through other things God has done, said, and shown you that point to the word you are waiting to see fulfilled. Go over your dreams from the last twelve to eighteen months, and find themes and key points. Gather together everything that addresses the specific thing God is telling you, and pray about it.

Many prophetic words are given in group settings and recorded. When you have discerned a prophecy is a real word from God, write it down—or at least write down the specific phrases God highlights to you. If you are part of a prophetic community, you could have multiple pieces of revelation from several different people. Bring them all together and consider them as a whole, as this will help you see the broader picture of what God is saying.

## Start Talking About the Word

Talking about a prophetic word is important because it builds your faith. It draws the word to the forefront of your mind and keeps it at the center of your thoughts. It is hard to forget or let go of a prophetic word if you are talking about it.

Some people believe that if we talk about what God is saying, this invites the enemy to resist the word and maybe keep it from happening. In my opinion, that belief gives the enemy far too much power. Anything God does the enemy will try to resist; that is just what happens. But we never need to be afraid that talking about a prophetic word will somehow give the enemy power in our life. God is much bigger than the enemy. If He doesn't want the enemy to know about something, He will just "veil" the revelation.

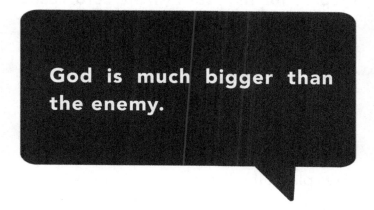

God is much bigger than the enemy.

He did it before:

> *But we impart a secret and hidden wisdom of God, which God decreed before the ages for our glory. None of the rulers of this age understood this, for if they had, they would not have crucified the Lord of glory. (1 Corinthians 2:7–8)*

When you know what God is saying to you, talk about it—to God, who will give you additional clarity, and to other people, who can encourage you and give you wise counsel and advice.

## Prepare for the Word (If the Lord Leads You to Do So)

When you have a good idea of where God is taking you, you will probably be able to see the "gaps" between where you are today and where you need to be when the word takes place. It is like what happened with me when I was a bank teller. I knew God was calling me to preach, so I needed to get better at preaching.

Do you need to prepare for what God has told you? Do you need to go to a certain school, apply for a mentorship, or develop your skillset in some other way?

## Regularly Check In with God About the Word

In the waiting process, be humble enough to ask the Lord, "Did I miss anything? Am I supposed to be doing something right now as I wait? Do I need to prepare? Is there something You want to change in my life? Is there something I need to learn? Does my mind need to change in some way? How do I respond to this word?"

If God doesn't clearly tell you what to do, it could be it isn't the right time yet, and you need to continue to wait. In this case, don't allow the enemy to push you into condemnation. "Well, you missed it. You're a failure. You're just a bad person. You're never going to walk into God's promise." Condemnation is about identity, whereas conviction is about an action. Conviction says, "Do this thing" or "Don't do this thing." There is a huge difference between condemnation (bad) and conviction (good). The enemy wants to make you miserable, but there is no condemnation for those who are in Christ Jesus (Romans 8:1). If something needs to change in your life, the Holy Spirit will tell you, especially if you are asking for His help. He is the One who lovingly and tenderly convicts you, and you have the privilege of following His voice.

Ask God to show you what to do, and don't let the enemy beat you up. If God gives you a clear answer, do what He says.

## Seek the Lord About the Timing

Timing can be a tricky thing with prophetic words. Many prophetic words take longer than we expect (though the opposite can be true as well).

God loves to help us get things right. If we are paying attention, we will often sense Him warning us of potential dangers like fears, distractions, opportunities that sound good but aren't what He has for us, etc.

> **God loves to help us get things right.**

He may give us clues about what to do when. In certain situations, I knew in advance that when a specific thing happened, it was time for me to move forward. In other situations, the opposite was true; I knew that when a certain thing happened, I needed to sit back and wait because it wasn't quite time for the word to come about.[12]

## Wage War with the Promises God Has Given You

> *This charge I entrust to you, Timothy, my child, in accordance with the prophecies previously made about you, that by them you may wage the good warfare, holding faith and a good conscience. (1 Timothy 1:18–19)*

Paul told Timothy to use his prophetic words

---

[12] *Sometimes God chooses not to warn people of mistakes, bad connections, painful friendships, etc. If this happens, it is always part of His plan. For example, if we make a mistake about what He is saying and go the wrong way, this could be exactly what we need to draw closer to Him and actually reach our destiny.*

to fight. When you know what the Lord is saying to you, you can pray into those words and use them as weapons of warfare. Begin to declare them over your life, specifically over the situation they apply to.[13] "Lord, You said this and I believe You." Fight the good fight.

Paul said Timothy needed to "hold" his faith. You can do the same thing. Hold fast to the prophetic word and to your trust that what God said will happen, even if it looks like the opposite is happening instead.

Joseph, Jacob's favored son, knew what it was like for the *opposite* of a word to happen. Through a dream, the Lord revealed to Joseph that his brothers and parents would bow down to him one day. Joseph shared

---

[13] *If you want to learn more about how to declare and wage war with your prophetic words, take a look at our online course called How to Craft Prophetic Declarations. We go through the specifics of crafting prophetic declarations and how to use them. What's the difference between a prophetic declaration and a faith declaration? What is declarative prayer? Do you know how to use revelation, Scripture, and testimonies to craft those things? This course is a whole lot of fun.*

the word, and his brothers eventually sold him into slavery, which in turn ended with his being thrown in prison for something he didn't do.

> *His feet were hurt with fetters;*
> *his neck was put in a collar of iron;*
> *until what he had said came to pass,*
> *the word of the LORD tested him.*
> *(Psalm 105:18–19)*

Hold fast to the prophetic word, even if it seems like it isn't happening, or the opposite is happening, because God *will* do what He said. When God says it, He will do it. He promises that a word from Him will fulfill its purpose!

> *So shall My word be that goes out from My mouth;*
> *it shall not return to Me empty,*
> *but it shall accomplish that which I purpose, and shall succeed in the thing for which I sent it. (Isaiah 55:11)*

## The Plan of God for You

Here are a few other things to keep in mind when a prophetic word feels slow to happen:

- If you have done the work and discerned the word is really from God, and you have received wise counsel from those you trust, hold fast to the word, and keep a good conscience.
- Make sure your heart is clean. Don't give in to despair, condemnation, shame, or (conversely) pride and arrogance.
- Do all you can to respond to God's invitation. Live in intimacy with Him, following His heart and His ways.
- Trust He will bring about what He promised. If He said it, He will do it. You have a real word from Him, and you can stand on it in faith.

When you know what God is saying, that word will become a foundation in your life, and no matter what happens, you will be able to hold on to it.

Later, as the word comes to pass—celebrate. Rejoice in God and what He has done, and tell the testimonies of His faithfulness. The simple practice of sharing your testimony builds strength. First, it builds *your* strength as you remember how He was faithful to you. If He was faithful then, He will be faithful now and in the future. Second, sharing your testimony also builds strength in those who hear your story. They will see at a deeper level how beautiful our God is. They will begin to long for His voice and have faith to step into what He is saying to them, because they saw you do it first. A single prophetic word can unlock more of God's purposes on the earth because of the testimony.

God has a plan for your life. He has something specific He created for you to do, and He is going to help you accomplish His plan. He will speak to you through prophetic words, dreams, visions, circumstances, Scripture, and more, and He will help guide you into that plan. Why? Because He loves you, and because His plan is the way you will feel fulfilled. It will help give you that sense of purpose and identity that every heart cries out for. We all want to know we are loved, that we are valuable, that we are important— and God gives us those things. They are found in His will.

As you learn how to discern His voice and respond to the prophetic words He gives you, you will step into that precious fulfillment and recognize you are helping expand His kingdom. It is growing in you and through you. As you realize this, your heart will be satisfied, *His* heart will be satisfied, and you will finally know what life is really about. All because of a prophetic word.

# ACKNOWLEDGMENTS

I have a debt of gratitude to the One Whose voice brought me back to life and taught my heart love. May multitudes encounter Your voice in that way!

To my wife, Dawna, who keeps showing me what it means to serve—your encouragement and prayers give me strength to be and do what God has called me to. Thank you!

To Streams Church, for being a family where we can work out together the implications of this life He has called us to. A people led by His voice, proclaiming His truth, and calling His children back home.

To Lauren Stinton, an extraordinary storyteller and editor that consistently makes me sound better than I should.

To Streams staff, past and present, who make projects like this possible. Thank you for your prayers, ideas, and hard work! Without you, Streams would not be what it is today.

# ABOUT THE AUTHOR

John and his wife, Dawna, were radically saved out of the drug culture in 1996. He quickly became interested in the prophetic, intimacy with Jesus, and the awe of God. With his background as a pastor and a minister in various settings around the world, John has a unique perspective on prophetic ministry and the global Body of Christ. He is the author of Dream Elements: An Alternative Dream Dictionary and the coauthor of The Art of Praying the Scriptures: A Fresh Look at Lectio Divina with John Paul Jackson. He has also written courses on prophetic ministry, dream interpretation, and other aspects of the kingdom of God. As president of Streams Ministries, he ministers internationally to help restore the awe of God to a world that has lost its wonder. He and Dawna live outside of Dallas, Texas.

StreamsMinistries.com
Facebook.com/streamsministriesintl/
Instagram.com/streams_ministries/
Youtube.com/@StreamsMinistriesIntl/

# ABOUT STREAMS

## OUR MISSION

Streams exists to reveal God's will to a world longing for hope by equipping believers to hear and understand God, fostering healthy prophetic ministry in local churches, and helping mature prophetic ministry into its potential.

We believe that every individual, church, ministry, business, and nation has a specific calling— something special and sacred—in God, and we get to help them discover and fulfill that calling as we teach about the awe of God and how to recognize what He is saying. Our goal is to encourage people to respond to His voice and fully expect Him to step in and do what cannot be done. We accomplish this goal in three ways.

## REVEALING GOD

We talk about God—how big He is, what He can do, His unlimited nature, His astounding love, His self-revelation in the coming of Jesus. We teach from the Bible about His nature and His ways. We demonstrate His love practically by serving the poor, encouraging those who are struggling, healing the sick, prophesying to those in need of revelation, and helping the oppressed find freedom.

## AWAKENING DREAMS

We train people in how to remember and understand their dreams. Though dream interpretation is a core facet of our ministry, we mean much more than just dreams in the night. We also help people awaken to what God was dreaming about them before the world began (Eph. 1:3–6; 2:10). We address and minister to that cry for significance and purpose that haunts every person until they discover for themselves the genius of God's plan for their lives.

## CHANGING LIVES

As we encounter God, learn how to respond to Him, and experience His true nature, everything changes. As we recognize how involved He really is in our lives and the world around us, we start seeing Him everywhere. As we experience the depth of His love for us, we come alive — chains fall off, weakness becomes just an opportunity for His strength, and faith becomes normal.

## STAY CONNECTED

 Streams Ministries, Intl.

Available in App Stores

# BUNDLE

To complete your Discerning & Responding To Prophecies set, be sure to order the Bundle. This Bundle includes the Discerning & Responding to Prophecies e-course and the Tips for Receiving a Prophetic Word study card. With this Bundle, you'll gain a deeper knowledge of distinguishing prophetic words you've received and further discover how to react to them effectively!

Scan the Qr code to order now.

# STREAMS ACADEMY

God is endlessly inviting us deeper into His world, and in His wisdom, He has designed us to discover His heart and ways together, igniting courage, inspiration, faith, and fresh insight for powerful breakthroughs. Streams Academy Prophetic & Revelatory Training is designed to plunge you into the deep and exhilarating waters of revelation. You'll learn and practice essential skills to fine-tune your ability to hear God and increase your understanding. Online meetings with other students and teachers will be held to discuss what you've learned to help you apply it to your life and propel you toward your destiny.

Scan the Qr code to join now.

# MORE RESOURCES

## By John E. Thomas

Like what you just read? Why not take a deeper dive into John E. Thomas' other resources? You can access more valuable information by purchasing either the bundle or individual resources.

Scan the Qr code to get today.

Made in the USA
Columbia, SC
07 August 2024